MW00880983

MY DADA
AND ME

By David E. Yeates
and Duchess E. Yeates
Illustrated by i Cenizal

Tellwell Talent
www.tellwell.ca

ISBN
978-0-2288-2106-9 (Hardcover)
978-0-2288-2105-2 (Paperback)

Hi. My name is Duchess. I want to tell you about my days with my Dada. I love him so much and he loves me too. He is my king and I am his princess.

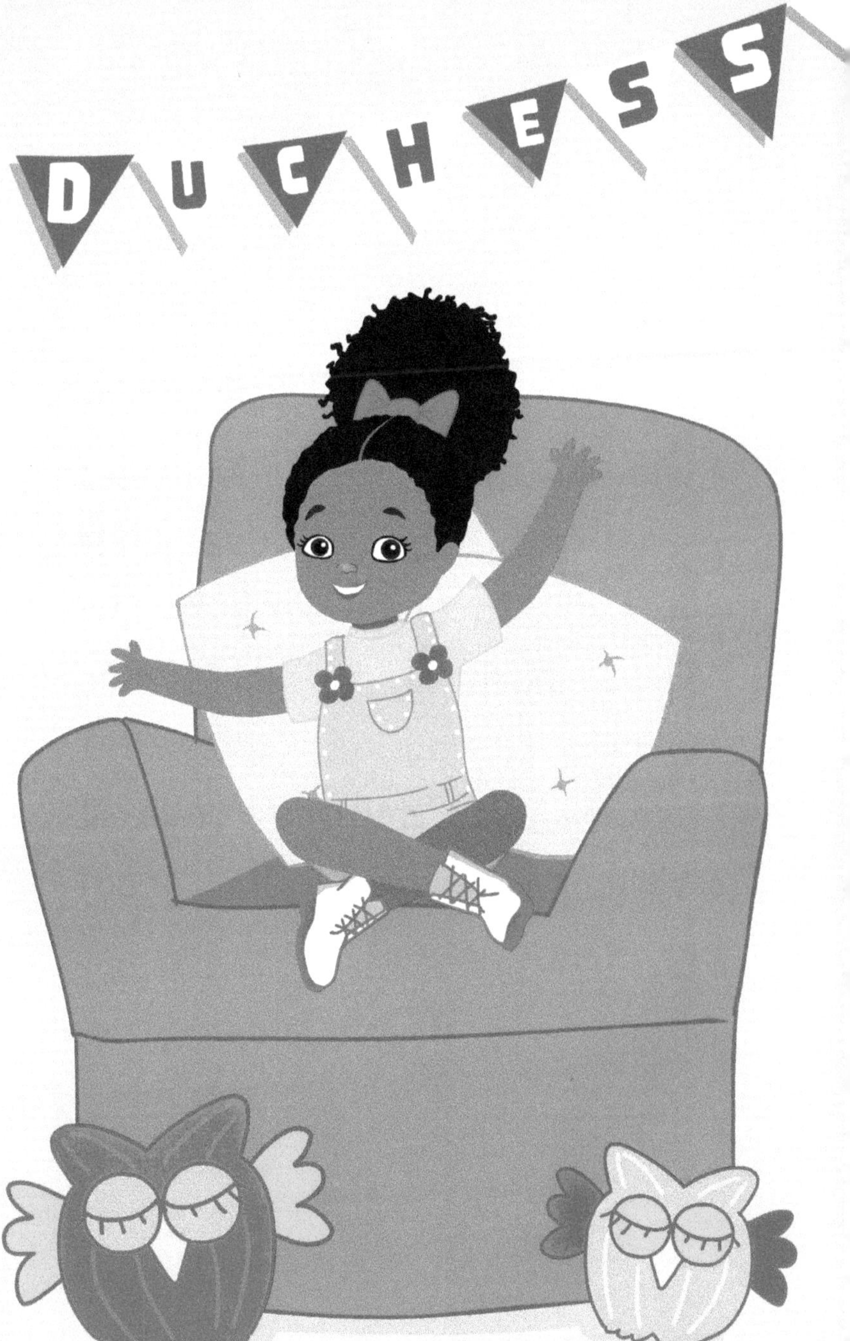
DUCHESS

Every morning, my Dada wakes me up with hugs and kisses. He sings my favorite song to me: "Good morning to you, Good morning to you." As soon as I open my eyes, my Dada says, "I love you, Duchess," with a great big smile.

When I sit up, I give my Dada hugs and kisses. I love when he squeezes me tight and picks me up out of bed.

My Dada carries me to the potty. Then he sings the "It's Potty Time" song to me. "It's potty time, pee, pee, pee, pee. It's potty time poo, poo, poo, poo." Then I finish using the potty and my Dada says, "I'm so proud of my big girl." He makes me feel so happy.

Next, my Dada prepares my toothbrush and sets the timer. Then, we brush our teeth together. I love when we dance while we brush our teeth.

My Dada asks, "What do you want for breakfast, beautiful?" I say, "Waffle, eggs, and oatmeal." They are our favorites. My Dada makes at least one of them for me every morning. My Dada loves when I have a lot of food on my plate. He says, "Wow, big girl, you eat more than I do!" I know my Dada is kidding because he has two waffles on his plate, hahaha!

Before my Dada and I eat, we say our prayers. I love it when my Dada says, "Aaaaamen!" I eat all of my food so that my Dada will be proud of me.

When I finish eating, my Dada and I clean our plates and wash our dishes.

Every morning, my Dada places three outfits on the bed and lets me choose my outfit of the day. My Dada always says, "Ooow, Duchess, Go Girl!" as he twirls me around in circles.

After I get dressed, it's off to preschool. My Dada always flies me around like I am an airplane before he buckles me in my car seat.

On the way to school, my Dada turns on the XM Radio to my favourite station: Kids Bop on channel 77. We sing our favorite songs together. I love when Dada lip-syncs to "Uptown Funk." It's so funny when he does dance moves while he drives.

When we arrive at preschool, my Dada always helps me get out of the car and puts me up over his shoulders for a piggy back ride all the way to my classroom.

Sometimes I don't want my Dada to leave, so I cry to him. My Dada always gives me a big hug and a kiss. Then he says, "You're a big girl, right?"

I say, "Yes," and then he hugs me and gives me lots of kisses until I am okay with him leaving. I do have fun at preschool and I like playing with my friends, but I often wonder what is Dada doing without me.

My Dada picks me up from school and takes me to the grocery store with him. I get to help him pick out items that we are cooking for tonight. Some nights we have dinner parties after school and I get to invite my favorite dolls.

Every day my Dada cooks dinner and I always help him. My favorite day is Taco Tuesday. I get to spread the cheese on the tacos. I always put extra cheese on my taco, because cheese is my favorite.

After dinner, my Dada helps me count my numbers and write my ABCs. He always tells me how proud of me he is when I count further than the day before. Yesterday I counted all the way to 30.

When we finish my numbers and ABCSs, my Dada runs my bath water. He puts bubblegum bath bombs and my bath toy animals in my water. I love when he sings the bath time song: "Splish, Splash, I was takin' a bath." I sing along with Dada until he leaves then I start making up my own words.

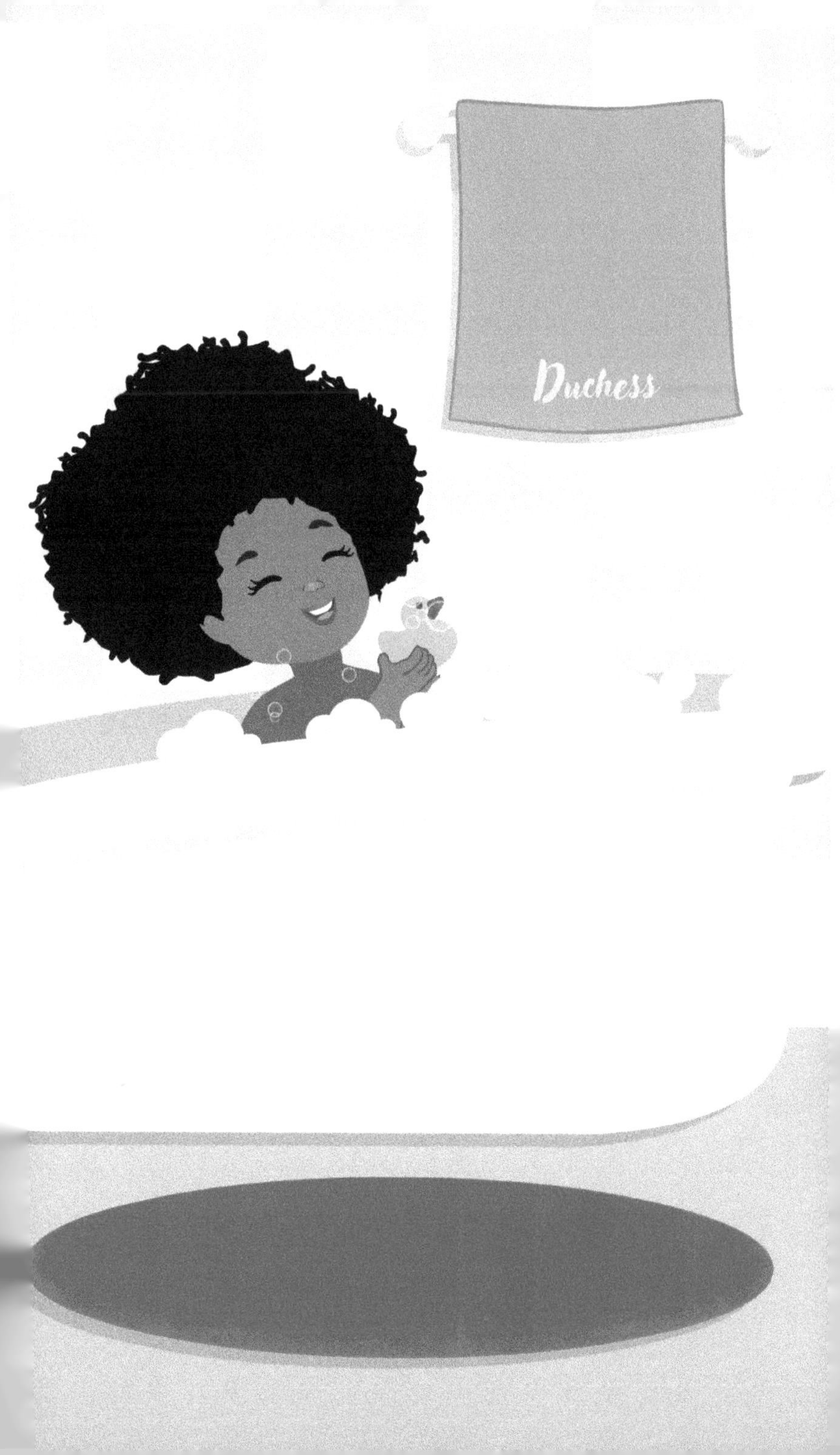
Duchess

When I'm all clean, my Dada dries me off and wraps me in a towel so I won't be cold. He always asks how do I put my night clothes on and I say "tag to the back!" My Dada says, "Duchess, you're so smart!"

After my bath, my Dada gets me ready for bed. We brush our teeth together and when I finish, he picks me up and flies me around the room over his head. I love when he does the crash landing in my bed. "Hahahaha!"

Some nights, my DaDa paints my toenails and my fingernails. I love when he pampers me. My Dada calls it spa nights.

Before sleepy, sleepy time, we say our prayers. I always ask God to bless my Dada and he asks God to bless his Duchess. We pray for our family and the world. Then Dada reads me a bedtime story. I love when he makes all the sounds and noises from the animal books. He always tells me he loves me and scratches my back until I fall asleep.

CPSIA information can be obtained
at www.ICGtesting.com
Printed in the USA
BVHW061827060421
604345BV00009B/937